D1361294

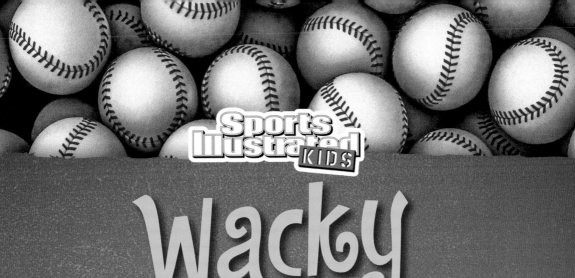

Wacky BASEBALL TRIVIA

Fun Facts for Every Fan

By Matt Chandler

CAPSTONE PRESS
a capstone imprint

Sports Illustrated Kids Wacky Sports Trivia is published by Capstone Press,
1710 Roe Crest Drive, North Mankato, Minnesota 56003.
www.mycapstone.com

Library of Congress Cataloging-in-Publication Data
Names: Chandler, Matt.
Title: Wacky baseball trivia : fun facts for every fan / by Matt Chandler.
Description: North Mankato, Minnesota : An imprint of Capstone Press, [2017]
Series: Sports Illustrated Kids. Wacky Sports Trivia
Includes bibliographical references and index.
Identifiers: LCCN 2015043261 |
ISBN 9781515719953 (Library Binding)
ISBN 9781515719991 (eBook PDF)
Subjects: LCSH: Baseball—Miscellanea—Juvenile literature.
Classification: LCC GV867.5 .C435 2017 | DDC 796.357—dc23
LC record available at http://lccn.loc.gov/2015043261

Editorial Credits
Brenda Haugen, editor; Terri Poburka, designer; Eric Gohl, media researcher;
Gene Bentdahl, production specialist

Photo Credits
Getty Images: B Bennett, 15, Diamond Images, 25 (bottom right), Lexington Herald-Leader,
14 (illustration), Transcendental Graphics, 11, Transcendental Graphics/Mark Rucker, 6;
Library of Congress: 5, 19 (Waddell), 25 (bottom left); Newscom: Icon SMI/Cliff Welch,
10, Icon SMI/Sporting News, 27, Reuters/John Gress, 28, ZUMA Press/Jim Thompson,
24-25 (top); Shutterstock: DutchScenery, 26 (moustache), GrandeDuc, cover, background
(throughout), Keith Publicover, 29 (deer), Marianne de Jong, 19 (marbles), matin, 4
(cabbage), 14 (cabbage), Milos Stojiljkovic, 8 (bulldozer), photastic, 7 (bat), 9, photka, 22
(toy), Piotr Marcinski, 18 (chicks), Podvamp, 17 (seagull), Tairy Greene, 4 (moustache),
Vladislav S, 7 (cork); Sports Illustrated: Al Tielemans, 13, Andy Hayt, 17 (Winfield),
Heinz Kluetmeier, 16, John Biever, 22 (Glavine), John G. Zimmerman, 18 (Campanella),
John Iacono, 12, 20, 21, 26 (Valentine), 29 (Wendell), John W. McDonough, 8 (Oswalt),
V.J. Lovero, 23

Printed in the United States of America.
032016   009682F16

★ Table of Contents ★

A LONG, WACKY HISTORY

Major League Baseball (MLB) is the oldest **professional** sport in the United States. Since the National League was formed in 1876, more than 18,000 men have put on MLB uniforms and earned money playing America's national pastime. From loony mascots to players with crazy **superstitions**, baseball has had many colorful characters over the last 140 years.

Why did Babe Ruth put cabbage on his head? Why did the owner of the Oakland Athletics hold a moustache-growing contest in spring training? How did a player get frostbite—in August? The answers to these questions and many more are all part of the wacky world of baseball trivia.

professional—a person who makes money by doing an activity that other people might do without pay

superstition—a belief that an action or an object can affect the outcome of a future event

THE BOYS OF SUMMER

About 750 players take the field on Opening Day in MLB. With in-season call-ups, more than 1,000 players could play in a season. That's more than 1,000 characters coming together in a competitive environment. Over a 162-game season, those players combine to create some of the wackiest stories in sports.

★★★ GIRL POWER ★★★

Babe Ruth and Lou Gehrig were two of the greatest hitters in the game. But that didn't stop a teenage girl named Jackie Mitchell from striking out the future Hall-of-Famers. It happened in 1931 during an **exhibition** game. A 17-year-old pitcher, Mitchell set down Ruth and Gehrig back-to-back in the game. She was only the second woman ever to sign a professional baseball contract at the time.

Lou Gehrig, Babe Ruth, and Jackie Mitchell

★★★ BELLE'S BAT ★★★

Indians slugger Albert Belle was known for hitting monster home runs. But Belle had some help along the way. He would use bats filled with cork in the center. Corked bats can make the ball travel much farther, but they are illegal in the major leagues. When Belle was accused of using a corked bat during a game in 1994, the umpire took the bat for further inspection. It was sent to the umpire's locker room. Belle's teammate Jason Grimsley climbed into the space above the stadium's ceiling and over to the clubhouse. He dropped down into the room and stole Belle's bat. He replaced it with a regular bat, but the umpire wasn't fooled. Belle was **suspended** for seven games, and Grimsley became the answer to another crazy baseball trivia question.

exhibition—a game played only for show; exhibition games do not count toward a team's ranking

suspend—to not allow a player to play or a coach to coach

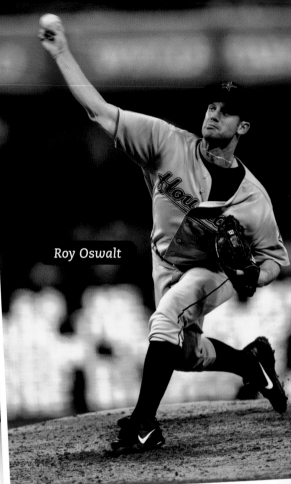

Roy Oswalt

★★★ DOZER DREAM ★★★

Baseball players are known to have strange **perks** written into their contracts. Astros pitcher Roy Oswalt's contract guaranteed him an unusual vehicle if he won a big playoff game. Oswalt had wanted a bulldozer since he was a child. So when he picked up the big win in 2005, the owner of the Astros purchased Oswalt his own Caterpillar dozer! Who needs a fancy sports car?

★★★ BAT MAN ★★★

Trades are an important part of baseball. Former Giants pitching **prospect** John Odom was part of possibly the wackiest trade in the history of the game. Players are usually traded for other players and sometimes for cash. But in 2008 Odom was traded for 10 baseball bats. The oddball trade earned Odom the nickname "Bat Man" among fans.

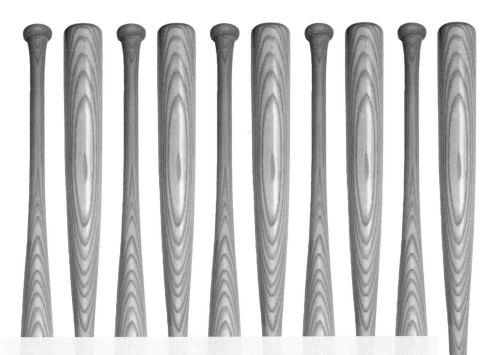

perk—an extra advantage that comes from doing a particular job or meeting a particular goal

prospect—a person who is likely to play professionally

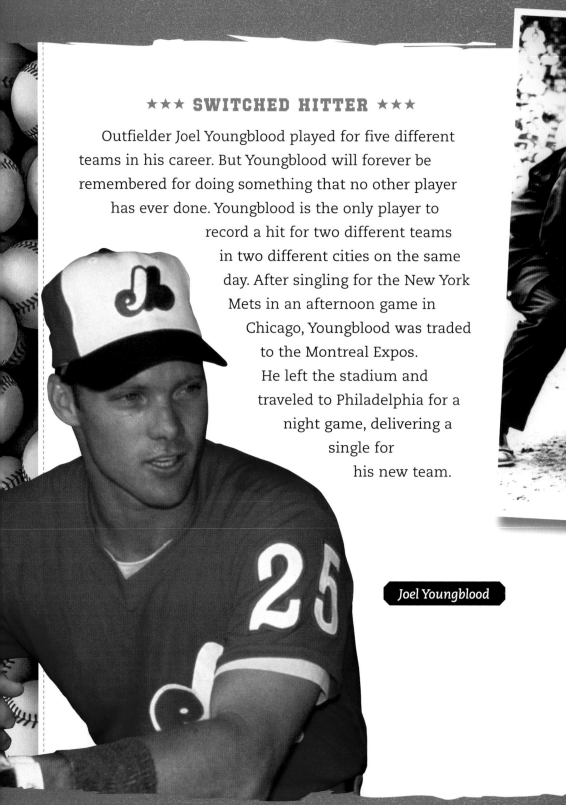

★★★ SWITCHED HITTER ★★★

Outfielder Joel Youngblood played for five different teams in his career. But Youngblood will forever be remembered for doing something that no other player has ever done. Youngblood is the only player to record a hit for two different teams in two different cities on the same day. After singling for the New York Mets in an afternoon game in Chicago, Youngblood was traded to the Montreal Expos. He left the stadium and traveled to Philadelphia for a night game, delivering a single for his new team.

Joel Youngblood

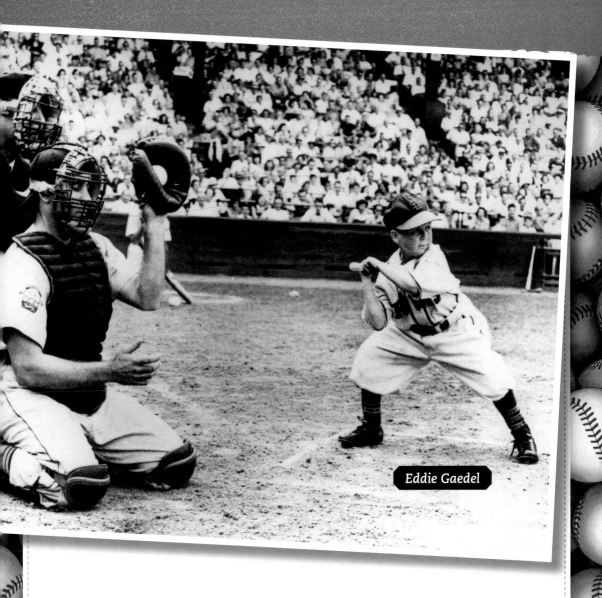

Eddie Gaedel

★★★ TINY BIG LEAGUER ★★★

Who was the shortest player ever to appear in a major league game? Eddie Gaedel, who stood just 3 feet and 7 inches (109 centimeters). He appeared in one game for the St. Louis Browns in 1951. He drew a walk in his only plate appearance.

★★★ AN AMAZING FEAT ★★★

In more than 200,000 major league games dating back to 1876, fewer than 300 no-hitters have been pitched. The no-hitter tossed on September 4, 1993, was rare for another reason. Yankee pitcher Jim Abbott shut out the Indians 4–0 without giving up a hit. Abbott was born with only one hand, but he didn't let that stop him from achieving greatness. To pitch, he would rest his glove on the end of his right arm as he wound up. Once he delivered the pitch, Abbott would quickly slide the glove onto his left hand, and he was ready to field his position.

Jim Abbott

UNUSUAL INJURY

★ ★ ★

Baseball is a physically demanding game filled with injuries. But only one player in major league history spent time on the **disabled list** (DL) because of a video game injury. Former Detroit Tigers pitcher Joel Zumaya could throw a baseball 100 miles (161 kilometers) per hour. But he was no match for a musical video game. Too much Guitar Hero play led to an arm injury and a trip to the DL for Zumaya in 2006.

Joel Zumaya

disabled list—a list of players who are hurt and can't play

Chapter 2

HALL OF FAME TRIVIA

Earning a place in the Baseball **Hall of Fame** is the highest honor for anyone who has played pro baseball. By 2016 only 312 people had been elected to the Hall of Fame. It's an honor given to only the best and most important people involved in the game of baseball. But that doesn't mean there aren't plenty of wacky personalities among those in the Hall of Fame. And with every wacky player comes some oddball trivia.

★★★ KEEPING COOL ★★★

What Hall of Fame pitcher wore a vegetable on his head during games? Babe Ruth liked to stay cool during hot games, so he would put two cold cabbage leaves under his hat. He would change them every few innings to stay cool.

HANDY PITCHER

★ ★ ★

Pitcher Greg Harris lost more games than he won during his 15-year major league career (74–90). Yet when he retired, the Hall of Fame in Cooperstown requested his playing glove. Harris was **ambidextrous** and had a special six-fingered glove that he could wear on either hand. In 1995 he became the first pitcher in the modern era to pitch left- and right-handed in the same inning.

Greg Harris

Hall of Fame—a place where people important to baseball are honored

ambidextrous—able to use both hands equally well

★★★ THAT'S COLD! ★★★

Future Hall of Fame speedster Rickey Henderson suffered one of the craziest injuries ever. He once missed several games because he developed a bad case of frostbite—in August! Henderson suffered the injury because he fell asleep with an ice pack on a sore ankle, and it led to a painful case of frostbite.

Rickey Henderson

Dave Winfield

★★★ DUCK! ★★★

Yankee superstar Dave Winfield was arrested in 1983 for something he did during a game against the Toronto Blue Jays. After warming up between innings in the outfield, Winfield threw the ball in, but it struck and killed a seagull. He was arrested and charged with animal cruelty. The incident was clearly an accident, and the charge was dropped the next day.

★★★ UNIQUE REWARD ★★★

What Hall of Fame catcher turned home runs into chickens in the 1940s? Roy Campanella is considered one of the greatest catchers to ever play the game. Before the Dodgers star made it to the big leagues, he was a power-hitting backstop in the minor leagues. One season a poultry dealer offered Campanella's team a unique reward. A player could earn 100 baby chicks for each home run he hit. Campanella smacked 13 long balls that year and collected 1,300 birds. He sent the chicks to his father to start a chicken farm.

Roy Campanella

EASILY DISTRACTED

★ ★ ★

What Hall of Fame pitcher once missed a game because he was outside the stadium playing marbles? George "Rube" Waddell was one of the best pitchers of his era. He led the American League in strikeouts six years in a row. But Rube was also known to miss games for odd reasons. Sometimes he stopped to play marbles with a group of children outside the ballpark. He also ran off the field in the middle of a game to chase a passing fire truck. Despite his oddities, Waddell was elected to the Hall of Fame in 1946.

George "Rube" Waddell

Chapter 3

SUPERSTITIOUS SUPERSTARS

Plenty of people believe in superstitions. Some may have lucky hats. Others might have favorite T-shirts they wear under their baseball uniforms for good luck. Baseball players are known to be some of the most superstitious athletes. With each superstition comes plenty of crazy stories.

CLOCK WATCHER

★ ★ ★

What former third baseman took batting practice at exactly 5:17 p.m. before every night game? Wade Boggs. Boggs had many other superstitions, including eating chicken every day as his pre-game meal.

Wade Boggs

Lenny Dykstra

★★★ GOOD-LUCK GLOVES ★★★

Center fielder Lenny Dykstra wore more than 3,000 pairs of batting gloves during his 12-year major league career. Dykstra believed when he made an out while batting, his gloves were partly to blame. After every out, he would get rid of the unlucky gloves and pull on a new pair for his next at-bat.

★★★ LUCKY NUMBERS ★★★

Some players believe their uniform numbers bring them good luck on the diamond. Really superstitious players will go to great lengths to keep their old numbers on their new teams. Which Braves pitcher paid to have a baby nursery built in a teammate's home in trade for getting number 47 when he joined the Mets? Pitcher Tom Glavine wanted to keep his luck going when he moved north to play for the Mets. For the lefty, having a nursery built for teammate Joe McEwing was a small price to pay for his lucky number. Other players have traded jersey numbers for vacations, expensive watches, and plenty of cold, hard cash.

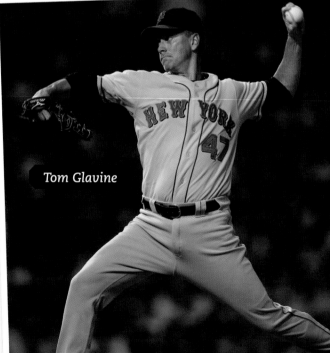

Tom Glavine

★★★ LUCKY MONKEY ★★★

Fans and players have long used the **rally** cap to bring struggling teams some good luck. With the home team down late in the game, fans will turn their caps inside out in an attempt to bring luck to their squad. Which team took it a step further and rallied behind a stuffed monkey? In 2000 the Anaheim Angels needed a rally or two. One day the scoreboard operator flashed a video of a dancing monkey on the screen with the words "Rally Monkey." Soon fans began bringing stuffed monkeys to Angels' games as good luck charms for their team. More than a decade later, hundreds of rally monkeys can still be seen at every Angels' home game if the home team needs a spark.

rally—to come from behind to tie or take the lead

Chapter 4

TEAM TRIVIA AND OUTRAGEOUS OWNERS

Fans come to the ballpark every night to watch the players perform, but the wackiness isn't limited to between the lines. MLB has a history of goofy owners and oddball managers. They all add up to some of the silliest stories in the game.

★★★ THE NAME GAME ★★★

The Albuquerque Isotopes are the Triple-A minor league affiliate of the Colorado Rockies. They may also be the only professional sports team to take their name from a television cartoon! The popular cartoon "The Simpsons" features a baseball team known as the Springfield Isotopes. Springfield is home to a nuclear power plant, and isotopes are chemical elements found in power plants. The real Isotopes don't have any connection to a power plant, just a wacky history of how they got their name.

★★★ BABE OR BROADWAY? ★★★

The Boston Red Sox created one of the wackiest bits of baseball trivia when they sold the contract of Babe Ruth to the rival New York Yankees. Selling a player's contract wasn't unusual, but that's only half of the story. Red Sox owner Harry Frazee sold the contract for $100,000 in 1920. Legend has it that Frazee needed the cash in part to put on a production of a Broadway musical, *No, No, Nanette*. Frazee thought the play would make him a pile of cash. Instead, the play bombed, and it would be 84 years before the Red Sox would win the World Series. The Yankees won four World Series titles with Babe Ruth on the roster.

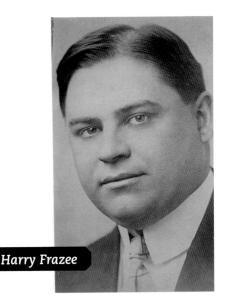

Harry Frazee

★★★ VALENTINE'S DISGUISE ★★★

What major league manager was **ejected** from his team's game and returned to the dugout in a disguise, including a fake moustache? Bobby Valentine, the former manager of the New York Mets. Valentine's trickery earned him a $5,000 fine and two-day suspension from Major League Baseball.

Bobby Valentine

THE MAKING OF A LEGEND

★ ★ ★

What team owner offered to pay his players to grow moustaches as a **gimmick** to sell more tickets? Charlie Finley. The creative owner of the Oakland Athletics offered $300 to each of his players and coaches to grow moustaches by Opening Day 1972. At the time only one player in the major leagues had a beard. None had moustaches, making the A's special—at least in Finley's mind. One member of the team was pitcher Rollie Fingers, who grew his now legendary handlebar moustache.

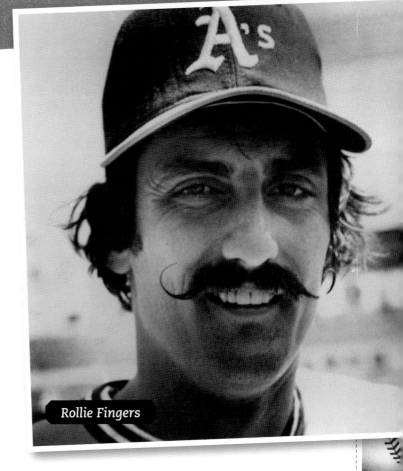

Rollie Fingers

eject—to force a player or coach to leave a game
gimmick—a clever trick or idea used to get people's attention

★★★ CUBS' CURSE ★★★

What city believes its team is cursed by a goat? Chicago is home to two major league teams, the White Sox and the Cubs. While the White Sox won the World Series in 2005, the Cubs have been in a bit of a dry spell. The Cubs appeared in 10 World Series' through the 1945 season. Then the curse was born. A local tavern owner tried to bring his pet goat to Game 4 of the 1945 World Series. When he was told the animal was not allowed, the man is said to have yelled, "The Cubs ain't gonna win no more!" Since the curse the Cubs have lost more games then they have won. And they have never returned to the World Series.

★★★ WILD TALES ★★★

Who knew there were so many wild characters in the game of baseball? For every tale in this book there are 100 more out there. Steve Lyons once slid headfirst into first base and then dropped his pants to clean out the dirt—in front of 30,000 fans! Yankee slugger Jason Giamba grew a moustache and his batting average jumped 80 points. Giamba gave all the credit to his new facial hair and refused to shave. And how about pitcher Turk Wendell? Wendell loved to hunt during the offseason. He was known to take the mound wearing a "good luck" necklace. The necklace was made of the bones and teeth of the animals he killed!

For a game built on statistics, the best trivia in baseball often has nothing to do with the numbers. Instead, it is all about the wacky personalities of the men who take the field.

★ Glossary ★

ambidextrous (am-bi-DEK-struhs)—able to use both hands equally well

disabled list (DISS-AY-buhld LIST)—a list of players who are hurt and can't play

eject (ee-JEKT)—to force a player or coach to leave a game

exhibition (ek-suh-BI-shuhn)—a game played only for show; exhibition games do not count toward a team's ranking

gimmick (GIM-ik)—a clever trick or idea used to get people's attention

Hall of Fame (HAWL UV FAYM)—a place where people important to baseball are honored

perk (PURK)—an extra advantage that comes from doing a particular job or meeting a particular goal

professional (pruh-FESH-uh-nuhl)—a person who makes money by doing an activity that other people might do without pay

prospect (PRAH-spekt)—a person who is likely to play professionally

rally (RAL-ee)—to come from behind to tie or take the lead

superstition (soo-pur-STI-shuhn)—a belief that an action or an object can affect the outcome of a future event

suspend (suh-SPEND)—to not allow a player to play or coach to coach

★ Read More ★

Editors of Sports Illustrated Kids Magazine. *Sports Illustrated Kids Full Count: Top 10 Lists of Everything in Baseball.* New York: Time Home Entertainment Inc., 2012.

Gitlin, Marty. *Baseball Legends in the Making.* Sports Illustrated Kids. Mankato, Minn.: Capstone Press, 2014.

Hetrick, Hans. *This Book's Got Game: A Collection of Awesome Sports Trivia.* Super Trivia Collection. Mankato, Minn.: Capstone Press. 2012.

★ Internet Sites ★

FactHound offers a safe, fun way to find Internet sites related to this book. All of the sites on FactHound have been researched by our staff.

Here's all you do:

Visit *www.facthound.com*

Type in this code: 9781515719953

Check out projects, games and lots more at
www.capstonekids.com

★ Index ★